Some Things I Do Not Know

Also by Arthur Allen

Here Birds Are
The Nurseryman
Treatments for Cut Flowers

Some Things
I Do Not Know

Arthur Allen

Shearsman Books

First published in the United Kingdom in 2026 by
Shearsman Books Ltd
PO Box 4239
Swindon
SN3 9FN

Shearsman Books Ltd Registered Office
30–31 St. James Place, Mangotsfield, Bristol BS16 9JB
(this address not for correspondence)

EU AUTHORISED REPRESENTATIVE:
Lightning Source France
1 Av. Johannes Gutenberg, 78310 Maurepas, France
Email: compliance@lightningsource.fr

ISBN 978-1-83738-036-7

Contents

I
SOME THINGS I DO NOT KNOW

Some things I do not know 9
Coda 27
Some things I hadn't told you yet 28
Seen / Un 31
The Turning Year 32
On Loughrigg 36
Calendar 37

II
THE ANIMALS
(An Intermission)

Sensitive Creatures 41
Ratlets 44

III
HAVOC

Buzzcut 55
The Dream Procession 56
No Body Here 58
Overnight 59
Mori Yoshitoshi 61
The Question of Suffering 63
Addiction Studies 64
[Unfathomable] 66
Of Note 67
Of Time 69
The Name of the Venom 71

Obituary 73
I could understand a little 74
Vanitas Portrait in a Two-Way Mirror 79
Of Course 82
Sober Diary / Alphabetical 85
The Art of Scraping your Grinder 87
How not to beleaguer the net for its holes 88
[I reread my first poetry book tonight] 90
Coup de Grâce 93

Acknowledgements 97

I

Some Things I Do Not Know

These poems owe their lives
to the death of a great friend.

One who died
Following
intricate song's lost measure
H.D.

Some things I do not know

This story
cannot be told right.
I know so very little.

I.

I do not know the number. I do not know the name
of the hotel in Lyon, but I would like to go
up to the desk and say: you hosted a death
here, in early December. That room, please.

I want to see the patterns on the ceiling,
the industrial light fittings, the curling plaster,
the generic canvas, the distant Rhône.
I want to see the last things he saw in this world,
if he saw at all. If he was looking.

II.

On google maps, the arrondissement
is palm-of-the-hand sized
from above; from the street it is
implausibly vast and teeming with hotels.

III.

I do not know
if there was or was not
a day of advent between

instant online booking
and your presence
in the room.

How the corridor could not

even be contemplated. How pure
orientation towards your goal
moved you down a passage
without value.

How you forgot
that the path is the goal.

How,
even in the interstices,
there was no time to pause

in silence and stillness too vast
for alternatives.

How any hesitation
could have broken your heart,
or perverted your action.

I do not know

how you moved –
strong and certain
as a cutting horse, or

if there was or was not
a single motion of Samba

isolated in a chain-gang
of purposeful striding
from the elevator door
to the mouth of the dolmen.

IV.

I do not know how

there was a moment
when the hotel-room door shut

and you never opened it again,
nor any other.

(The time of the eschaton
came and went
while it was closing.)

The unhurried hydraulic action
of the fire door, a measure of safety,

containing you
like a fire. Four

chosen walls, or more –
it may not have been four.

The stock-image
in my mind says: yes, but
I do not know

into what you walled yourself
like an anchorite,
bricked in to die
like Robin Hood.

V.

Did you let yourself
enjoy some final things
or think it better not
to risk a single pleasure?

If you allowed yourself to drink or eat
on your last night on earth –

I do not know.

But I do know you. Naturally
ascetic and self-flagellating,
I think you won't have eaten
(fear of indignity, maybe).

Stomach: vacant, radiant, glistering
sense of star-filled night
under the solar plexus.

Heart: full and fast-beating like a hunted mammal
or a hedgerow bird, wing-pinioned
in the crowded centre of closed hands.

(I want to say a mouse's heart,
but I think you would not like the heraldry.
A hare might do. But the heart was yours.)

Cold winter water
within. No anxiety. No
fear of dawn.

I do not know how

a sense of armistice was cast
like light about the axis
of your woundless body.

VI.

If you moved on the bed
like a shark in harbour,
how you passed the time
that would have passed in any case.

I do not know

how you folded up your hardy cord
trousers like the leaves of a wintering plant,

how you left
your halo and your sceptre
balanced on them.

I do not know,
when you turned off the light,
if there was still light
from the city, or the sky,

or if your feet really were bare
or where you were –

Where were you?

I do not know how
you were cloistered in darkness,
a density of darkness
from which you did not rise.

How you lay down, lamb-eyed,
long as the minute hand, and dark, and still.

The laid-down stillness of the tomb
at Arundel and older,
the way the eldest of our tribes
waited in tunnels of stone

(still, and still moving,
founding habits in their blood)

for the catch, the hunt, the loss
to come to them, far in
under char and ochre animals
and the pelt of the rock.

I do not know how
you shut and locked like a knife –
above or below the bedsheets?

VII.

How
could you not be seduced
to one last sin

of caring?

That you could leave me
so ignorant of the hour

when no living creature
could have intervened

by coming in the window,
resting its forehead in your palm.

Predators calm in the face of an early owl,
or the sudden cat's sharp hiss: *Don't*!

"Life is short, but art is long.
Suffer on", says Tove Jansson.

The sprite-eyed island face of Jansson
could not have changed your mind?

Nor glowing moth, nor curious
squeaking mammal witness from
behind the wainscot?

Stop me if I turn histrionic.

I know, it isn't merciful to show your workings.
I know, it is all the same suffering song. But:

the window and the sky at night
had no surprises left for you.

This you believed so
fervently, you made it true.
I do not know how

no resource of love
could keep you.
I do not know if,

at final bite of gloom,

a solitary bird did come, a bird
that does not herald happiness.

VIII.

I do not know how
often you rehearsed,

how brave you were,
and / or patient,

how your great task
surrendered in your hands –

like a bird about to be saved
from the confines of a home?

How there was or was no
sense of déjà vu or doubletake,

a drop beyond which you had to act
as if you were still choosing,

though you had a choice no longer.

How you did not need a sign,
nor wait for one – that you'd decided
was enough of a sign.

I do not know how

the moment before held
          like a tiny blue egg

suspended among rain
and wind and pine trunks.

Nest above, roots below.
Falling, not fallen.

Hold on that frame until
the projector's beam burns through.

IX.

What we call dying is simply the last pain.

I do not know how

your final irritation was soothed
till it became a static hum, a softening

of eyes – of everything that drove you
closing, throughout your body.

If sleep came soft as mist
at first, then heavy,

like snow
falling within you,
blanketing the routes

till your blood in its channels
slowed and gelled and curled.

Till all your inner animals lay down and sighed,
their yokes and bridles vanished,
their ploughs and whips shed in the harvest.

Astonishing
how wide awake you were
up until then.

X.

I do not know

how
at a moment you
barely determined

the softest separation occurred, like mist parting from mist.

How you muttered
or did not mutter: *all shall be well,*

and tighter knotted the stems
of your determination

(my fine black orchid
in a hand-built greenhouse
of Romantic agony).

I do not know
how you drew in death like a cigarette

but I remember the way
we used to smoke for mercy

and autonomy, we said, for grace
and amnesty, for a moment

when even the forgetting is forgotten.

XI.

Novissima hora est
May there have been
just a lightness.

May death have arrived as unawareness:
painless, insentient, creeping peace

like the endless moment before
waking from a blameless faint.

I do not know how
all life dared
to keep on moving

even as your last breath touched
the corners of the room,
                                        as it turned

to less than dust on the pillow.
        So many of us lived on –

and death, which happens always
to someone else,

        happened to you,
above or below the blankets.

May it have been under them.

XII.

Thirty summers ended,
I do not know how.

I do not know if
there was a lesson

on the threshold
as the stars regained you,

you who were
ever wary of the lore
about going home.

I do not know if

you came apart like a conifer,
thinning
needle by needle.

What did you think at last?

Don't tell me. I'd rather die
than know.

XIII.

How your body cooled
the air about it like a river,

after. If, after
morning came,

the dawn staggered,

appalled to waste its light
on your closed,
no longer sleeping, eyes.

I would have sung – I don't know what,
but I would have sung to save you.

I would have bound your wrists
with my hair.
          Any of us would.

CODA

About my poems, you always said,
I never knew when to end things.

And you were right –
I don't.

Will you tell me
when it's finished?

Distal moonrise.
Clouded moon.

Let all this be something,
though

where you are now
I cannot even dream.

charged with knowledge
knowing nothing
W.S. Merwin

Some things I hadn't told you yet

You left us in the pentad
when the tachibana first turns yellow,
and I write to you now

from the micro-season
when the pheasant first calls.

It is the beginning of midwinter.
The seasons are working on us,

inseparable from our own workings.
And the first pheasant calls.

Surely, the seventy-two pentads were familiar?
If not, you would approve, or pretend to

already know – and you wouldn't rate
the app that tells me this!

The seasonal fish of the pentad
your faithful correspondent
is currently in:
                        cod.

The kanji character
is built of two components:
          fish and snow.

Did you know that?
Wouldn't it have pleased us both
for me to tell you?

Everything I hadn't told you yet
(the sort of things you'd really like)
havocs and drifts between my ears.

Listen:

I want to say, as if I've always known,
how in Tibetan *alaya* means 'home',
and *himalaya* means 'home of snow'.

Listen:

I want to speak of Alan Watts,
about one of his chosen paradises:

a shop on Tera-Machi in Kyoto
that sells incense, writing brushes, ink.
Watts goes there to buy aloeswood
(which, as Dr. Suzuki told him,
has the essential smell of Buddhism).

Last time,
he found a small stick
of vermilion ink
sheltered in gold leaf.

It must be mixed
on a windowsill,
early in the morning, with a dewdrop
for the water.

But what he found this time,
you will never know.

Yoga
interrupted by the postman
bringing a note
meant only for me.

        Tears.

My non-absorbent yoga mat preserves them
perfectly
like dew in the morning.

Ink could be mixed here. But it is not.
Instead, a kind of clay develops –

skeins of dead skin combine with tears
into a base material
at the foot of my vision,

forward-folded as I am
by the all the things I hadn't told you,
and haven't made into a poem.

There is no telling now, which is also to say,
there is no knowing anymore.

How could you have thought your search was over?

This dewdrop world—
Is a dewdrop world,
And yet, and yet…
Kobayashi Issa

Seen / Un

Walk weeping up my favourite hill
listening to the music of Sorrentino films.

Hardly a soul about,
myself
hardly a soul at all.

Open Instagram
to write to him: I love you.

Can't. Can't tolerate that
my words be left unseen.

*

Two little hearts,

lodged like stars on the margin-edge
of my final messages,

appeared naturally
overnight, a week ago,

like red apples set by summer
on the apple boughs.

"Miss you"; "We must go to Naples"
Seen

The Turning Year

I.

    After five years
it has come back to a Saturday

G-
my father,

who I cannot see
and cannot turn my mind from –

how can we have been without you
        for so long?

    After five years,
what my heart disbelieves
        it disbelieves a little less.

The feast day of our dead is the 23rd of January

(Bedgebury Forest,
accident without substance,
                    9° centigrade).

        Mum plans her feast:

"Steak. Crème fraîche, with peppercorns. Slice
up an onion. That's what G- … that's what we did.

But I don't think
I'll do all that just for myself
                    ."

II.

In my memory
you are using up your life,

growing straight into death
like a daylily in the slow attrition of a day.

Your body I remember
as the calmest of things,

laid out long and useless
like the standing leg of a flamingo.

Your silence confounds me.
That it is continuous
hurts me daily.

Maybe you don't remember that
the voice of my society
was born of your mouth.

III.

Let today in like a dog that followed us
down the beach and cried

on the stoop of the holiday cottage:
tristesse, blind trust, sunlight.

One day – maybe soon –
I will see what has happened now
has happened for good

and I'll walk with it like a dog-not-for-keeping,
saying, "We can only be this close.

(Pause)

Thank you."

IV.

Recall you as a star
falling like it was made for falling.

A star that knows the path ahead
and no road home.

After five years,
then, it has come back
to a Saturday.

Down here,
someone is still
belting out the song you sang:
And la la la la la la la la means I love you.

N– says *I can't believe it's been so long*
and *I almost feel I've been on my own forever.*

On Loughrigg

I.

Our path,
a watercourse
the pearl-grey colour of pear.

An autumn lake
is drubbing the fells,

        watering
the ancient Briton under the hill,
under harebell and bristling restharrow.

II.

What was falling without ending
lifts suddenly away.

Fugitive streams
vanish like snakes
into the moorland;

rain and people rest under the same quilt.

            Hidden in the wind
like birdsong on the mountain,

we climb
bright emptinesses,
stepping over lost rivers:

their tails and their long cascades
shrink between the terrier's paws,

washing unseen fossils on their way
down to a level where the earth remembers
    times before flowers.

III.

Out of breath
behind my mum
in sudden rain –
it is her birthday.

Autumn rain
that feels more like the rain of spring.

Calendar

Now I must write
your death-poem

(must I?)
It begins:

        Midwinter.

        Night.

and ends:

        ...unfinished dreams.

[and ends every winter, and every winter ends,
and the grief-work never ends, the work begins again
without ever having ended on the 5th of December
(before bears retreat to their dens,
                                        before the salmon spawn)
and again, in late January, savagely,
when the giant butterbur flowers
and mountain streams freeze over,
and – regular as clockwork – my father dies once more.]

II

The Animals

(An Intermission)

Sensitive Creatures

I

K– called: he had inside news: nationwide lockdown would be announced at 17:00 – he had to go to Lidl right now, it was 16:32. We walked down Easter Road like we were chopping it for firewood. K– didn't share his intimations but wore them from head to toe; he could see animals fighting in the distance, fighting in the aisles. Frenzy showing the tips of its ears. We had barely taken the bottom branches off Easter Road when we were heralded in a loud voice by a man who needed to move every one of his bags and cases to the other side of a side street, like a riddle with a fox and chickens and a river, and could we help him. Our shoes put down their axes. He had a dark ochre matter building at the corner of his mouth like a god who has been talking for a long time in a workshop of earthy dust. I don't believe he had a home.

II

His belongings – ceramic plates, cracked, mosaiced with fishbones; sleeping bag, moving and rustling like a dreaming body; roll-mat; clothes, thin, plaid, not clean; and many open jars – had all been ferried over the road-river. K– looked up hopefully, like a nice sky. He was still alive with the law of urgency, its one command: to panic buy. But we were told now to bring the things in behind a blue door, the man said he had permission, and K– was only a little triumphant when he said that it was locked, it must be, it was a front door, but he had only assumed. I pushed it, it opened: "Oh ye of little faith", the stranger said. "Sorry, God", I thought, and we began the second riddle of carrying into a dull and sleeping stairwell.

"Now. Down the stairs," he said, and "Tuck them far away."

III

There were enough possessions that it took the two of us several journeys, fully laden, and the man stayed always without. At the head of the stairs on the third trip, a black case burst open in K–'s arms like a puppy waking. He had to sift and pull the contents back together with his bare susceptible hands; his mouth made a tight undulating line, like ants form to cross the jungle. Regaining the stairs as he shot the clasps home, I felt for a moment that he might kiss the luggage with unrestrained passion like the head of Saint John the Baptist, but he just hove it before him in both hands; these he used afterwards as though they were no longer his, keeping them always at arm's length.

IV

We arranged the assorted possessions like a woodpile with the bark side out to keep off the worst of the weather, and, fairly pleased with our work, emerged on the road to find the figure in whose employ we had been labouring gone. It's okay to feel relief sometimes, particularly if you need to get to the supermarket and your foreman-like G-d is nowhere to be found and your work seems to be done and has seemed to be done before but now must truly be over.

V

The Lidl on Easter Road is larger than any other Lidl I know, by two escalators. I've never been in another Lidl that contains an escalator. This gives the Lidl on Easter Road a futuristic quality like the Tokyo Solamachi, which means Skytree. I read this morning it is the tallest building in Japan; contained in it are over three hundred stores and also the Sumida Aquarium, where "sensitive creatures are starting to hide". The grass eels have become ill at ease; except their keepers they don't see anybody, they have started forgetting about humans and human faces. They are even hiding from their keepers now. "Here is an urgent request," the aquarium wrote, "could you show your face

to our garden of eels
from your home?"

The event will be called a "face-showing festival".

VI

We are rushing face-first towards Lidl. And before you know it the escalator is propelling us higher up and farther in like telepresence robots that have just graduated from the University of Tokyo, spilling towards Sumida Aquarium to show the grass eels their honours and ribbons, their certificates and beaming human faces.

Ratlets
or 13 Views of the Killing of the Rats

[1]
In the basement, resting the barrel
on an ironing board, I drew a horned man
in purple crayon, shot it between the eyes,
then went upstairs and killed the rat.

The trees made note of this:
that many beasts feasted in the garden
where they all eat – in safety,
with their hands – in the same way

but only one
warm-blooded thing
was killed that morning.

[2]
The sight was in its centre
so I may have closed my eyes
in the final moment
of drawing in the trigger.

The safety caught:
a small white circle
signifying, momentarily,
                    pause.

I pushed it home,
like bolting a back door,
and shot. It screamed,
it ran. I did not see

where it ceased to move
among dense lilac leaves
that hummed with foul power,
like wild garlic in woodland.

[3]
The purpose
that had borne me
into the final moment

left
when I leapt ashore
from the good ship Lethality,
        me its fatal figurehead.

            Came to the body this way: as though
I had been following the traces of a beast
that had turned on its traces and, facing me,
was filling up the tunnel I crept down,
equal in breadth and height to my fear.

Half-saw and half-created
a soul-shaped rodent
rising without loyalty
from the body into verdure,
reproachful, unreproachful.

Felt triumphant
                        revulsion only.

Worse only had it lived on,
impenetrably trembling
and uttering the doglike
whimper of chipmunks
who have been betrayed.

[4]
My father-in-law asked,
"Are those your gardening gloves?"
"My executioner's gloves", I said.

[5]
Approach the body like a deer
I have lost the right to shoot.
The boughs scrutinise me as
I bend over the foot-sized body.

I had shot quicker than thinking,
but when I picked it up
by the waist, I thought:
'I have killed him,'
and it made me want to cry.

[6]
A grip relaxes on the garden:
the ferns begin again to show
their tender faces; each
needle and leaf-vein brims.
A chipmunk finds my hand.

          My father-in-law
smiles over his frontier,
now unburdened

of the biblical fear – pestilent mammals –
that drove him to Canadian Tire
in search of the junior-sized air-rifle
               I am clutching.

[7]

I hold it in pretence of knowingness,
wishing secretly it were made of wood:
flintlock, ramrod and black powder,
but the stock and barrel are matte black plastic,
synthetic and skeletonized in 'tactical-style'
like a part from a child's toy Batmobile.

The chassis is compact, designed
specifically for 11–15-year-olds.
The calibre is .177, it shoots
at 495 feet per second (five
below the requirement for a licence).
        Ambidextrous
        automatic safety
above and behind the barrel
like a star.

[8]
At the precipice
I must tell myself:
This rat has no wit.
And hold my gun very carefully.[1]

[1] Comrade Mao Tsetung's concept, outlined in his *Problems of Strategy in China's Revolutionary War,* says: "Our strategy is 'pit one against ten' and our tactics are 'pit ten against one' – this is one of our fundamental principles for gaining mastery over the enemy." There is not a single thing in the world which is not a unity of opposites, which is without a dual nature. Strategically you must deride your adversary, whilst tactically taking them seriously. Real tigers are paper tigers at the same time. "This is a Marxist-Leninist theoretical generalisation of great profundity" (*Stories About Not Being Afraid of Ghosts,* 10).

My throat
prepares a squawk
like a single pale firework,
dares not release it.

The rat leaps
like a flame; the cloth
of its flank tears
with a snap.

For a moment, it seems to be dancing.
        But it is not dancing.

[9]
Threshold of fir trees
quivering with vigilance.
Birds and chipmunks flee,
scramble into the soil,
the sky then wheel about
in blue-dark hollows,
shouting their panic, accusation:
   Was it me? Us?
              Was it one of us?

The grackle turns back
   with a whale's eye,
      small and cold.

The cardinals, no longer dumb,
their voices salmoning, count themselves
over and over in hysteria of survival.

[10]
Went holding the rifle wistfully,
listless limb bereft of purpose,

body
(draped like rag
across my palm)
a metric weight
not even an extra-tough
thorn-resistant Marigold
could disguise.

[11]
Over McCafé at the drive-thru,
I told Pat all about it, with a woundedness
appropriate to the hunter who kills.

Three crows come to see Pat regularly
and he feeds them mice on a bloody stone;
his father keeps a crossbow in the bathroom;
I knew he'd understand. He said,
"Eric McLuhan terms rage the soft
belly of male boredom,"

said he would offer the rats to the crows
and the crows would eat them cheerfully.

[12]
(Later, the two bodies
side by side like duellists
under the weight of the day.

I stand by them.
The racoons steer clear.

Do not leave me all alone with the dead, Henri Michaux
like a soldier at the front who gets no mail.)

[13]
Spotted while on the phone to an uncle.
Hove the rifle by its barrel, hoisted,
hardened shoulder, aimed and fired.
I had thought it only one, but
it bifurcated among the fronds.

Fast action.
Tentative confidence
my veteran hand
might have had
appeared wrong.

Later,
found the intended pellet
rolling loosely on the sunlit rug

(to know what occurs in the painter's head,
follow their hand).

It looked like a seed or a flowerhead shaped like a dancer,
its pleated lead skirt and cupola
an impossibly light and fatal bellflower.

From Canadian Tire
I remember:

a heavy pellet in a low-powered airgun
gives a trajectory that arcs like a rainbow.

How it might have
ended: simply
and ideally,
the garden valley
singing a plain *Amen.*

But afterwards
the whole setting
is enormously empty.

III

Havoc

If I am pressed to say why I loved him,
I feel it can only be explained by replying:
"Because it was he; because it was I."

Michel de Montaigne, on his best friend,
Étienne de La Boétie, *Essays* (1580).

Buzzcut

When you got that buzzcut
should I have thought more about it?

So little between your brain and the world:
taut skin and skull above, your thoughts
moving just below – exposed so the sun could watch

the blood arrive to nurse the grubs of your ideas,
your closing arguments. It seemed like you
were showing off the cage, and, somewhere,

a bird was silent. Shocking how monk-like
it made you: devotee of a private chapter,
an order of one. An ominous sign –

like when the feng shui master tells you
the city on the mountain nearby is greater
and shaped like a fishing net,
and your city is shaped like a fish.

The Dream Procession

Below the peaks of Le Glandasse,
the chantry was closed. I could not see you.

My monument was made with West Sands –
the sea has ground it out already –
but here comes the procession:

Down the coffin-road,
          blindfolded horses
                    draw your coffin.

Seven thousand cattle, precisely those which
founded the El Paso (with a hundred and thirty settlers),
bristle and low as they compass the horizon.

Aurochs (the same that crossed the ice bridge)
kneed the skyline with their shoulders.
Pampas cats and nocturnal dogs come in pairs

to nuzzle and cry at its edges: the litter
of osier twigs and ocote and girders of candlewood,
thorned to protect flamenco-scarlet flowers.

Pashminas and rebozos threaded with gold
flashing lamé swaddle the rigid form,
                                                            I cannot
                                                                        describe

beneath the shroud. The good-looking corpse,
disfigured only by lifelessness, as he willed.

The humans among us go
slowly, leading the horses.
We will sleep on our feet and eat,

in the turning night, tacos
of bull testicle and blood sausage
and tell no stories but to animals.

*

Seabed feeling of the land –
a stripped, salt-scoured emptiness

and something about the air
as if it all had been underwater,

studded with birds of prey,
of song, wheeling like mobiles.

Our bowed heads follow the azimuth
unswervingly. We walk the ceaseless ground
where your feet belong.

Scorpions and snakes are nowhere seen,
even once the procession gets moving,
begins to weave itself into the dust;

scorpions and snakes are concerned
with strangers in their locus,
and there are no strangers here.

Friend, move with us. Forget with us
the ancient fealty to one place.
To one landscape, one graveyard.

No Body Here

I am groping in the dark for a body
kept from me by time and distance.

                    Your body,
where you staged a losing battle,
overnight retreat (tactical withdrawal).

                    Your body
of martensitic steel that breaks
just as jaggedly but less often, and,
as with any blade, breaks but once.

Which you tended faithfully and then unpeopled.

Now, you have no body on earth but ours.
No hands but ours, no feet but ours, and
it is our eyes you must look through now.

Our books that you must write.

Overnight

Shock of the empty plinth,
                                        the vacant frame.

You were given an important place in my life
and departed from it without a word,

ground to nothing in the mill of the night.
My constant marvel over

how much you could get done overnight

(the right five thousand words,
          or endless reels
of twelve-beat compás

conjured
as if you worked
in praise of darkness)

has finally been exhausted.
Before dawn,
you submitted yourself to death

satisfied, at least, to have crossed
nearly everything off
your last to-do list.

Make sure
you are quite finished dying:

          strikethrough.

In Time's sentence
we take our places like commas,
while, in order to end it, you
have immobilized yourself into a period.
Cioran

Mori Yoshitoshi

was the first to find his grandfather
(the second hereditary head
of a school for wooden flute)

who had committed hari-kari in an upper room,
his body painted hurriedly with the flag of Japan
in its centre, and still growing.

I'm sorry for whoever found you:
orderly, immaculate, not outwardly injured,
young, good-looking
                    and beyond repair.

Mori used to hum *nagauta* – songs
composed to accompany kabuki dances,
performed after tragic scenes, and said to help
"magically uplift an audiences saddened hearts."

From the mouth of his mother and his aunt
they were Mori's childhood lullabies.

Across the whole career of his printmaking,
Mori returns to an archetypal instant in kabuki:
the moment when fate changes,
                    the last possible moment.

Several of his stencils bear the title:

        'Just a Moment'

Only a face,
fiercely framed
in a mask of armour,

carved by knife on a woodblock.
A warrior's face, and a warrior's command
that halts fate.

The Question of Suffering

He would make life difficult for himself
when he wanted his life to be difficult.
And never failed

to write me smugly from a stalling night bus
or while sifting the red dirt of the shoulder
where his motorbike went under
like a poached deer near Bogotá.

But living with malady
involves health and sickness
at once:

"This minute I was well,
        and am ill,
                this minute",

wrote John Donne from the sickbed of 1624
where he believed his was a fatal illness.

Addiction Studies

Study 1.

Relentless narcotism.
Flick the leeches
from my window;
they fall, glowing.

My thoughts cannot be trusted
and nor could yours.
I have even thought of Jesus.

Study 2.

In the muffled middle dark,
our favourite drug pressed
like a flower between
the hard black carapaces
of our lungs, we used

to remind each other:
Nothing in nature lives on smoke.

Study 3.

Inhalation as a suckling
child on a mother of smoke
milk of smoke
mother of fire (& marijuana)

Study 4.

In the long dark
petal-closed nights

in the cold of the world
thoughts last years

and I cannot
let your death alone.

The scorpion is drinking his venom again,
is drunk on it, and chanting:

repeat exposure
will dull the sting of anything.

Lord, deliver him.
From the sins that are past;
From Thy frown and Thine ire;
From the perils of dying;
From any complying
With sin, or denying
His God, or relying
On self, at the last
John Henry Newman

•

Unfathomable,
and final as the verdict
of papal astronomers
– the *why* of another mind.

Of Note

Your bloodless note
I won't discuss

more than to say:
perfunctory.

Void
of nostalgic detours,

lacking even
in mystery.

Nothing to express, and no
means of expressing it.

There was room for a P.S.
There wasn't one.

Later

[The card itself means something. One of Kuniyoshi's hungry ghosts, stolen from the giftshop where I worked in Oxford,

but the envelope
means more than anything:

my address,
my name, his writing.

And within it, all this accusatory space. I accuse it
of ambivalence, of certainty, of double-speak, of emptiness
sans luminosity, and it does not, cannot, refuse my charges.]

Of Time

You are no longer
among the flowering neck-
deep nettle garden where,
seven years ago, I treated you
as if you were still happy, such
that you almost were.

Where you alighted on the line
from Dickman or Dickman:

"Shaving my father's face
I'm not shaving
my face
I'm shaving my brain"

Shaving my brain. You liked that.
A nice, clean-edged brain.
Pruned, sheared, and coppiced.

I see you clearly in the years of May-
day, and me beside you: two
happy Pinocchios, both knowing
they had found a brother, and perhaps,
secretly, a new Geppetto.

How often we stood
keyless, before the locked
doors inside each other –
but it means something
for two friends to rest their foreheads
flush to those unopenable edges.

Though we have passed out of earshot
of the song of those days –

fording the Isis with books
clutched like children in your arms,
shirtless, clearing a garden of nettles
in the carefree book of summer –

we were right *here*.

The Name of the Venom

I.

stayed potent and small
as a mustard seed.

A proper noun
preserved –

the seed of death,
embryonic, but complete.

An engraved stone
washed in a secret chamber

of your heart.

                    Of any heart,
an ending can be arranged by accurate

admix of hairy willowherb,
or inexact of Ambien, or anything

designed to cause injuries
incompatible with life.

        In St Andrews, in another decade,
you overheard the name of a barbituric ester,

smuggled it off like a jewel beneath a hat,
or else it clung, a lethal limpet.

In any case, you could not
have forgotten nor
dislodged it, had you tried.

II.

Suffering checked in, seeking the boon
of oblivion in his inside pocket.

From there it called like an arrowhead,
as if the weapons of war should
themselves arrive seeking blood.

So it happened. So, it happened.
Enough, then. Never mind its name.

Obituary

He will not suffer
an exhumation here,
and what would I say anyway?

In love with my own partial view,
I arrange my pietà
without Peter: body or spirit.

You can cradle someone without all that.

I could understand a little

Triumph of your disconnection:

escaping
by means of catastrophe
you were spared

infirmity and the long injustice
of ageing, the slow leak, forever bailing,
and the squandered, pedestrian voyage of years.

Some vanity there.
Body-fat-ratio fixed for good
against the hopelessness

of elapsing time, the inexorable losing,
how nothing is ever itself again.

If it was that sense of ruin
which is worse than pain,

I could understand a little.

Or fear of doldrums

Fear of forgetting your childhood,
of having nothing but your childhood.

Of becoming someone,
no-one.

Fear of the dragging
antlion den of the world.

The pain of making
every choice –

Thoughts like these,
        I could understand a little.

If you felt incapable
of being yourself
and also loving yourself.

(Plath letter, Feb 4
1963, bastardised)

If you passed the slaves of money in their districts,
and felt that you, too, were a slave,
just to much less money.

If you dared to want (in this world
                                that is a dream of wanting)
and everything you wanted seemed to you null.

A faded copy of the 1969 summer bulletin
of California's revolutionary Mid-peninsula Free University
reads: 'The natural state of man is ecstatic wonder,
                                we should not settle for less.'

If you felt you were forever settling
for less,

that your work was just rearranging
ikebana of dead and dying flowers,

I would remind you to be grateful
but I could understand – a little.

If it was exhaustion at the endless mornings:
dread and loneliness, regardless of company,
human or literary, in blind-laddered light.

If the thought was: I will always be
remembered as I was.

I would not call you selfish. I read somewhere
to be afraid is to continually think of yourself.

E.g. the blear condensation in the car windows
that felt like my fault, the fault of my breath,
although I couldn't help but breathe.

I could understand a little
if it was something like that, but you never quite said

and even if you had
it would have only been one

scuff of hoofprints
from the landscape of your thoughts.

I could have held your head
while everything rose away

like you once relaxed against me
veiled in the dark
labyrinth of Vondelpark,

and though I could understand
my presence would have been illegal
if you'd shared your plan,
and you never asked.

Vanitas Portrait in a Two-Way Mirror

I cannot describe him
to you or a stranger.
I will:

He was my brother.
I lost him.

Dark-eyed
land-lubbed sailor,
seen always at a distance,
and walking away. Black-plumed

poet-child, armed with disdain
against the consciousness of misery.
With rituals to keep him safe, to keep him feeling
safe, whatever the weather: safety or danger.

The idea of dying was with him
continuous as the idea of himself.

Bone structure
of Hungarian vizsla
stretching under
the face of a melancholy seiner
husbanding the mud plain

– have you seen him?

He was not trying to deceive anyone
really, he was only struggling
to come to terms with his own negotiators.

Unsettling genius creature, unsettled
by a ravening emptiness
in the halls and nooks of himself
and a black wind on the fellsides.

He thought he owed himself a death,
and paid in full by long drawn plan,
leaving so much Fuentes still unread,
so much Márquez, and many more

examples of how to live in noble exile
against the indignity of the world.

Victim of his own exacting
intelligence, of a lucidity
which smothered him.

My co-seer and conspirator of arching
eyebrows. The other half of all my winks.

He could not prefer
the absurdity of living
to the absurdity of not living.

My deadly, only once
defeated, dueller.

A boy out of time,
like an artist growing up
in the shadow of bygone Edo.

I used to think
we would become
strangely good people.

I should have been able to manage
something more like you than this egocentric monologue,
but accept it for friendship's sake.
W.H. Auden

Of Course

Swim down.   Breathe out.   This is
                                   true apostasy.

Don't panic. It is too late.
Remember, if you can,
the end of choice   was all you wanted.

Close your eyes.   It is time to learn

how the natural state of eyes is closed.

You may feel like a chestnut horse
is running suddenly beneath you.

        Do not reign it in.
This is a moment of crucial passage,

but not the final crossing. That is over water,
always.
        A moment of clear water:
                    no before, no after.

You are beyond the duality of wet and dry
but I'm glad you've dubbined your boots.

We're all very impressed with the care you've given
your boots, now forget them.
                    Reason ends

                    here. That's right,
through the ogival door.

Fear is usual, at the threshold
hesitation   is the form of movement,
but you are beyond coming or going.

Within and without are no longer.
Vertigo is natural.   The depth unfathomable.

All metrics fail.

Forget about your wisdom,
your visions and attempts.
                        Bow with courage.

We have prayed for you
                                    who had not strength to pray.

Let us reassure you, as you are,
that your death was always a part of your life
and there is no final judgement,

not even from those on earth.

The situation you are in
is itself profound enough
to be regarded as knowledge.

You
will not be used to feeling
so unlike yourself –

to find your taut edges
          drifting out like pollen

magnetised towards forebears
you do not recognise as human.

Ah, you have found the ballroom mirror
– shards, of course – but here you lived

another life, loved
without knowing it, in a thousand fragments

of memory and dream, between Kerala and Santiago,
and Edinburgh and Reims. How brilliantly

you dwelt there in those silver slivers, held
without knowing it, reflected without vanity,
so close, so nearly as you are,

but still, of course, the object
of all those other
imaginations.

Now
take my hand
as if we are in separate bodies.

Here is fire,
without its light.

There is the blue gate.
There the second page of life.

Sober Diary

Nothing for three days.

Well, I've scraped my grinder till I could see unpainted metal and grew concerned about my lungs being lacerated with sharp silver dust. But I've bought nothing, ground nothing. Brittle with restlessness that is not quite energy, feeling the evening yaw around me. Before it's eight o'clock, I've laid out all possible preparations for tomorrow's breakfast. Tidal changes in the brain: just pick up, there's nothing left of today to corrupt. Just don't. You will not feel better. Ease is not the same as health, or betterment. Betterment. What the fuck does that mean? An advance that is also a return. A return of what? A self I remember, a way of being I just about remember, but our previous selves do not return. They cannot. Every atom has altered since, has been remade. Betterment: an upward spiral, somehow. But there's hours of this evening still to go! If I walk to Lidl and buy some eggs, I will already have replaced the eggs I'm yet to poach and eat tomorrow. Feels insane to do that. I'm definitely going to. Because I have a favourite stupor that I must not acquiesce to. Yes, I'm about to walk to Lidl to replace a box of eggs I won't finish till tomorrow. But I have also written down this, which is more than nothing, is the face of the fact of a beginning.

Alphabetical Sober Diary

A return of what? A self I remember, a way of being I just about remember, but our previous selves do not return. An advance that is also a return. Because I have a favourite stupor that I must not acquiesce to. Before it's eight o'clock, I've laid out all possible preparations for tomorrow's breakfast.
Betterment. Betterment: an upward spiral, somehow. Brittle with restlessness that is not quite energy, feeling the evening yaw around me. But I've bought nothing, ground nothing. But there's hours of this evening still to go! But I have also written down this, which is more than nothing, is the face of the fact of a beginning. Ease is not the same as health, or betterment. Every atom has altered since, has been remade. Feels insane to do that. If I walk to Lidl and buy some eggs, I will already have replaced the eggs I'm yet to poach and eat tomorrow. I'm definitely going to. Just don't. Nothing for three days.
They cannot. Tidal changes in the brain: just pick up, there's nothing left of today to corrupt. Well, I've scraped my grinder till I could see unpainted metal and grew concerned about my lungs being lacerated with sharp silver dust. What the fuck does that mean? Yes, I'm about to walk to Lidl to replace a box of eggs I won't finish till tomorrow. You will not feel better.

The Art of Scraping your Grinder

You know it better than anyone: its shape,
its mechanism. You know where compacted clods cling,
where the residue has built up limpet clumps
at the base of the teeth, plastered the curved wall
in dark impasto. All this can be eroded,

and brushed free. Deploy the blunt side
of nail scissors rather than the sharp
(more purchase, fewer plastic slivers).
The faces of the teeth – parallelograms
plus tumulus – provide rich pickings, too.

Bend your head in an attitude of prayer;
attend patiently, under strong light,
like a painting conservator, a watch-
maker. For a time, there is the sense
you could scrape and brush forever, the way

numbers can be halved infinitely, but,
before long, the task gets thankless, the dregs
exhausted. Put it in an inaccessible
cupboard, intend, firmly, to go without –
or, at least, to go without for a while.

How not to beleaguer the net for its holes

Language permits us to see
Carlos Fuentes

But do not look too far ahead,
or trust too much
in the proper name of anything.

All things change
beneath their names,
        and living can mean
so many awful things.

But you loved words –
patina, scuttle, y, chamois –
and, more than that,
you sought their ends.

What do they net anyway?
Not the flesh you really had.
Not your (secret,
                and self-secret) thoughts.

Disciple of the Janus words,
the contranyms,
you never forgot a synonym
of 'protected' is 'endangered',

or how *Weather* means both
to withstand and wear away,
Left to remain and depart,
Cleave both to cling and to hew,

Original both first
creation and new invention.

(See also: *bound,*
bolt, buckle,
dust, hold, fast.)

And *last* can mean either
final or most recent
(as in 'Krapp's Last Tape').

Was there no word left
to parry with you?

•

I reread my first poetry book tonight.

He and I were in it together:
after the great loss, right at the start,

Pierre was there, in Amsterdam.
I quoted him there, on the page, and I'm so glad
I make poems out of real life, with love, in real time.

We hung in the nets of the playground
in Vondelpark like flies,
and he, thinking of his room in Oxford, said

spiders bite me every single night and I know
where they live but I don't want to kill them.

          Thank god
my poems are not poems.

And you will never know
how all that remains
must flower

in your absence, must feed
on the warm dark mulch –

will flower   will feed

(transubstantiation into nature –
a classic of poetic closure).

Yes, we have gone on
into the here-after,
now-ever, your afterlife

within us
but not ours
on Earth, where we are

perpetually at the start of our story
that is destined to last till the end of our days.

We come from everything, abide in
          everything, and return to everything
                    from which we were never parted.

But how to believe any of this?

I write it down, I repeat it aloud,
earning no comfort and rest
reciting this poem.

The cat is turning felt
back into wool with playful fury.

She looks over like a Buddha,
infernally content.

(O my teacher of crazy wisdom)

P----- A------ Z---- ended.
By his own arrangement. The Alps disappeared forever.
Latin America too. India. Memorious dust.

What happened to everything?

You asked for it to end
and it is over.

Coup de Grâce

Now
you are a story

forever
already finished.

Worry about nothing.

Sylvia Plath
(letter to her mother)

I write without seeing. I came. I wanted to kiss your hand. […]

This is the first time I have ever written in the dark […] not knowing whether I am indeed forming letters.

Wherever there will be nothing, read that I love you.

Denis Diderot, Letter to Sophie Volland, June 10, 1759.

Acknowledgements

Thanks to Shearsman, and to Tony Frazer for considering and re-considering this book.

Thank you to the editors of journals in which poems from this collection first appeared, including 'Ratlets' in *Vocal Inhabitants*, the 2025 anthology from Strange Region Press, 'Buzzcut' in the New Zealand Poetry Society Anthology for 2024, and 'Dream Procession' in the iOTA centenary issue.

Some Things I Do Not Know was chosen as a finalist in the Snow-bound Chapbook Award, and shortlisted for the Cinnamon Press Literary Awards, the Templar Poetry Pamphlet Awards, the Alastair Reid Pamphlet Prize and the Live Canon Collection Prize. Poems from this book have been longlisted for the Plaza Poetry Prize, the Live Canon Poetry Competition and the National Poetry Competition.

Thanks to everyone who supported this project and responded to earlier drafts of these poems, especially to Dr Miriam Gamble, for her tolerance and for the sharpness of her tools.

For their continued participation in my work, for never quite falling silent, I will thank the dead whenever I see them – Graham Allen, Wendy Partridge, Pierre Zahnd.

And, finally, any acknowledgements page is incomplete if it does not mention my indispensable partner, Ashleigh Trickett; her dexterity, her curiosity, and her care. And my mother, Nicki Allen, to whom everything is owed.

www.ingramcontent.com/pod-product-compliance
Ingram Content Group UK Ltd.
Pitfield, Milton Keynes, MK11 3LW, UK
UKHW010916040326
468628UK00002B/167

9 781837 380367